MW00768799

My Vision Journal

A Guided Journal to Assist in the Manifestation of One's Dreams

Copyright ©2013 by Aishah Tatum

Published in the United States
ISBN: 978-1981681464

The Journal is dedicated to the best in all of humanity. It is my sincere hope and prayer that this journal helps you to become all that you are capable of becoming.

Aishah Tatum

I dedicate this Journal to all of the women seeking to Live Fearless, Fulfilled and Fabulous lives. The women who want to show up every day as their Authentic Selves & Live their God Given Destiny.

For You, Mom

Property Of

_____

Contents

What is a vision journal?

A vision journal is a journal that is designed to assist in the creative process of mani-festing ones dreams. It allows one to go within and tap into the limitless boundaries of their imagination in order to attract to them what it is they see in their minds eye. Vision journals are also designed to help one remove false beliefs hidden in your subconscious mind. Sub-conscious beliefs, whether true or false, will create your experiences. These beliefs will con-tinue to affect your reality and experiences until you change them. Vision journals integrate the power of affirmations, meditations, imagery, and inspiration and are created to help you focus only on your dreams, write about the feelings of achieving those dreams and experi-ence the feelings of living your dreams right now in the present moment. This Vision Journal will help you to bring harmony, health, wealth, and happiness into every area of your life if you use it.

How to use a Vision Journal

Vision Journals should be utilized at least three times daily, in the morning, mid-day, and before bed time. You do not need to spend an hour each time, only about 10-15 minutes 3 times a day. Upon awakening, we recommend opening the vision journal to your gratitude page, after you have spent a few moments thinking, feeling, and speaking gratitude turn your attention to any image in your vision journal. Focus on the feelings of having this image in your life, see it, feel it, taste it, smell it, and imagine yourself with it. It is extremely impor-tant that you add as much sensory information to your visualization experience as possible. Spend at least 60 seconds on each visualization.

Next, we recommend saying your affirmations. Say your affirmation until you feel and believe that what you are wanting is definitely yours and is in the process of coming to you. You will also find an action list for each visualization. Spend some time writing down at some point during the day what action you will take or took to make the vision a reality. Lastly, we suggest giving thanks to The Creator for what you have asked for, you surely will receive, as long as you believe.

Last Tips before beginning your Journal

Vision Journals are personal books that should be kept private. No one should see your vision journal except for you unless you want them too. Remember though that it is very imperative that you do not share your visions with people until they manifest because they loose energy and attracting power when you speak of them over and over again to people. It is important in the creative process to keep your attention only on what you desire. If you are around negative people, please remove yourself from there presence. If you watch the news a lot, or a significant amount of TV, please reduce this amount greatly unless what you are watching is positive and uplifting. We also recommend some sort of exercise and a healthy change in food consumption during this time as well. Even if you only drink 1 extra glass of water daily, or begin to walk for 5 minutes daily while reciting your affirmations this is fine. Remember that EVERYTHING has a vibrational frequency and you only want to attract positive vibrations that will bring harmony in your life.

What are Affirmations?

Affirmations are positive statements that you send out into the universe with feeling and belief that will attract to you what you are affirming. Affirmations are also statements that we make to ourselves, either intentionally or unintentionally. Affirmations affect the emotional state of mind that we are in and they affect our conscious and subconscious mind. Affirmations coupled with visualization increase the power of belief that we have in what we are wanting which brings things to us even faster.

Writing Affirmations:

Affirmations should always be in the present tense. You never want to say affirma-tions in the past tense because you want your mind to think that what you are saying is taking place now.

Write each of your affirmations down on paper at least 20-25 times and try to write these affirmations in the first, second and third person. For example, "I, Martin, am a healthy young man". "Martin, you are a healthy, young man." " Martin is a healthy, young man." Affirmations should be written as if what you are wanting is taking place or has already taken place in your life. For example, "I am Healthy" is more powerful than, "I will be healthy". Affirmations should always be positive statements and contain positive words or phrases. For example, " I am no longer in debt" is an example of a negative affirmation, although you are telling yourself you are no longer in debt, your mind hears and thinks debt. Instead, try, " I am financially free", or " I am wealthy,". All three phrases are similar, however, the positive statements include the belief that you are no longer in debt, if you are financially free.

Also, Use your own style of language to write and say your affirmations. For example, one person may write an affirmation that says, "It is my divine birthright to receive all of my hearts de-sires," you on the other hand may say, " I was born to be happy and I deserve any and every-thing I ask for." Remember Affirmations should be believable for you. Say your affirmations aloud at least 3 times per day and each time say them at least 5 times before you proceed to the next affirmation.

If you are in a situation where you can not say your affirmations aloud, then say them to your self silently over and over again throughout the day. We recommend that you keep your vision journal with you during the day so that you can use it as often as you can, and keep your mind and thoughts focused on what you are wanting. You may want to keep your vision journal in your car, your office, or your back pack during the day.

Some examples of Affirmations are listed below:

Self Image/Self Esteem: I am a beautiful, healthy, and loving Person.

Weight loss: I eat only healthy and nutritious foods. I now weigh_____ . I am always able to maintain my ideal weight.

Wealth: I am wealthy beyond measure. Everything I do brings success to myself and others.

Health: I have perfect health.

Relationships: I am in a loving, romantic, monogamous, and fulfilling relationship with_____. We enjoy each others company and love spending time together.

Peace & Harmony in your life: I am always in harmony with the uni-verse

For Depression: I attract only joy and happiness into my life

Fear & Anxiety: I am confident. I release all negative emotions.

What is Visualization?

Visualization is the process by which one uses mental imagery, positive affirmations, and sensory imagery (taste, touch, sound, and hearing) to create positive and lasting changes in ones life. When we visualize we use our imagination to create a clear image, idea, or feel-ing of something we want to manifest in your life. What you form in your minds eye, your imagination, is as real as the air you breathe. What we envision already exists in the invisible inner world of the universe. What we imagine already exists in our minds.

How to Visualize

There is no right way to visualize because each individual is different. Some people are able to create clear images in their mind because they are visual learners, others may need to "feel" the feelings of having, doing, or being what they desire in order to manifest, and others may just begin to expect what they want and show gratitude for it while thinking about it. The most important thing is that you create the feeling place of what you desire constantly think about and give thanks for it and expect it. Look at the pictures you have in your vision journal and then close your eyes and try to imagine that you have the very thing that you are seeing.

To demonstrate how easy it is to imagine, lets go through one exercise.

There is a room with 4 walls. Each wall is painted a different color. The wall in front of you is bright pink, the wall to your left is bright yellow, the wall to your right is bright green, and the wall behind you is bright orange. There is a huge window on the wall in front of you. When looking through the window, you can see an ocean with clear blue water, a low tide. There is also a blue bird standing on the sand next to a sand castle. The sun is bright orange and you can hear the sounds of the ocean and the birds chirping in the air. You ap-proach the window and open it to find a nice cool and calm breeze touch your face and flow through your hair. Now open your eyes. It may be helpful to write what you want in the vi-sion journal with as many visionary and sensory details as possible and then close your eyes and imagine what you have written.

Simplifying the Law of Attraction

Everything that exists in the universe is made up of energy. We are all energy and everything that we see and don't see is made up of energy. Everything in the universe has a vibrational frequency. Thoughts are energy. Our organs are energy. The book you are reading right now is made up of energy. The food that you eat is energy. Thoughts and feelings have their own energy that attracts similar energy vibrations that exist in the universe.

Everything that exists, exist first as a thought. We always attract into our lives what we focus on the most, believe about the most, imagine most vividly, and expect the most. What we think about, believe about, and feel on the most intense levels we will bring into our lives.

Principles of the Law of Attraction

Remember that thoughts have an energy that attract like energy

The best way to guide this energy is by doing the following:

1. Know clearly what your heart desires and ask the Creator for it.

2. Focus your thoughts on what you desire with strong and intense feelings of enthusiasm and gratitude

3. Feel and Act as if the desire is already acquired

4. Be open to receive it

My Vision Journal

My Vision Journal

"

WE MUST REALIZE WHAT IS
ACTUALLY GOING ON BEFORE
WE CAN EFFECTIVELY DEAL
WITH IT.

_____

Ralpha

Chapter One

Life Assessment

Assess Your Life Now Section

Where are you now, Financially, Spiritually, Socially, Physically, Mental health, your emotional life, in your career?

Describe in detail your Life now?

What do you want to change about your life?

How are you going to change your life?

What are you going to do differently?

How are your relationships with yourself, your mate, your family, and your coworkers?

How are you managing your time?

How much effort are you putting in to reach your goals?

What areas of your life need improvement?

Life Assessment

Life Assessment

Life Assessment

_____
_____
_____
_____
_____
_____
_____
_____
_____
_____
_____
_____
_____
_____
_____
_____
_____
_____
_____
_____
_____
_____
_____
_____
_____

Life Assessment

_____
_____
_____
_____
_____
_____
_____
_____
_____
_____
_____
_____
_____
_____
_____
_____
_____
_____
_____
_____

Life Assessment

_____
_____
_____
_____
_____
_____
_____
_____
_____
_____
_____
_____
_____
_____
_____
_____
_____
_____
_____
_____
_____
_____
_____
_____

"

ACKNOWLEDGING THE GOOD THAT YOU ALREADY HAVE IN YOUR LIFE IS THE FOUNDATION OF ALL ABUNDANCE.

—

Eckhart Tolle

Chapter Two

Gratitude

My Gratitude Section

In this section of your vision journal you want to take some time to really think about all of the things that you are grateful for. Wheth-er small or large, write down all of the things that you feel grateful for in your own life. In this section feel free to put pictures of the things that you are grateful for and/or write out, "I am grateful for ...."

If you are grateful for your family, you may want to place a picture of your family in this section and write out, "I am grateful for my family, they love me and I love them". We STRONGLY recommend that you add to this list everyday why you work through your vision journal and read this section of your vision journal a few times per day. Even if you only take 60 seconds to read over the list, do it! Below are a few questions to help you get started.

Things to be Grateful For

1. Do you eat something on a daily basis?

2. Do you have the ability to drink clean water daily?

3. Do you have at least one pair of shoes? Clothes to wear?

4. Can you see the writing on this page?

5. Can you hear?

6. Do you have enough money for gas?

7. Are you able to walk?

8. Do you have a family to call or go home to?

9. Do you have a bed to sleep in at night?

10. Are you still breathing?

Gratitude

Gratitude

_____
_____
_____
_____
_____
_____
_____
_____
_____
_____
_____
_____
_____
_____
_____
_____
_____
_____
_____
_____
_____
_____
_____

Gratitude

Gratitude

Gratitude

_____
_____
_____
_____
_____
_____
_____
_____
_____
_____
_____
_____
_____
_____
_____
_____
_____
_____
_____
_____
_____
_____
_____
_____

"

AT ANY MOMENT YOU HAVE A
CHOICE THAT EITHER LEADS
YOU CLOSER TO YOUR SPIRIT
OR AWAY FROM IT.

———

Thich Nhat Hanh

Chapter Three

Spirituality

Spirituality Section

Spiritual growth results from absorbing and digesting the truth and putting it into practice in daily life-white eagle

Spirituality lies in the inner dimensions of ones self but is often times reflected in the outer conditions of ones life. Spirituality is the foundation of our beliefs, our values, and our character. Our level of spirituality is reflected in how we communicate with our self, others, and the world. It is also reflected in the choices that we make. Spirituality brings understanding, compassion, joy, and purpose to our lives. As we grow spiritually we begin to feel a sense of connection to all life, it awakens us to a divine presence in all creations. As we develop our spirituality we become more in tune with who we are and we have a better understanding of the beauty and gift of life itself. In this section you should focus on your spiritual development. Write down and answer the following questions to help you get started.

1.   What is spirituality to me?

2.   How is my spiritual life now?

3.   What areas of my spirituality do I need to focus on?

4.   How can I develop my spirituality?

5.   What is my idea or vision of a highly evolved spiritual being?

6.   Are religion and spirituality the same thing to me?

7.   Do I believe in Higher Power?

Spirituality

_____
_____
_____
_____
_____
_____
_____
_____
_____
_____
_____
_____
_____
_____
_____
_____
_____
_____
_____
_____
_____
_____
_____
_____
_____

Spirituality

Spirituality

Spirituality

Spirituality

"

THERE IS A POWER GREATER
THAN ME THAT LOVES ME
EXACTLY AS I AM.

———————

Unknown

Chapter Four

Self Esteem & Self love

Self Love Section

The way we see our self is far more important than how others see us. We as humans often times compare ourselves to others. We base our own self worth on these comparisons and on how others treat us. The most important thing to remember is that we are all great, worthy, brilliant, and beautiful in our own way. No two people are exactly alike. It is unfair to compare the outer images of another's life to your overall life. This is unhealthy and although not an excuse, you never know what that person is going through behind closed doors.

We all have inner struggles and weaknesses that we need to improve on. Also, we have to remember one very important thing, we are HUMAN. We are not perfect. We make mistakes. At times we beat ourselves up over things that we have no control over and other times we beat ourselves up about choices we may have made in the past. This tends to have such a negative effect on our psyche and how we feel about ourselves. Remember, the past is over; you did what you did because you thought it was best at that particular moment in time. Now as you look back on the experience, you realize that you could've done things a little different. It's ok. We all feel that way; this is what life is about. You live and you learn and you move on. Below is your self-assessment.

Take some time to answer these questions before moving forward. Remember, love yourself as you are and accept yourself and all of your imperfections now. You are on a journey of self-discovery.

1. How do I see myself?

2. How often to I compare myself to others?

3. What do I beat myself about?

4. Do I really love my self unconditionally?

5. What do I wish to change about myself in order to love myself com pletely?

6. How important are others opinions about me?

7. What do I regret?

8. From what you regret what did you learn?

9. Has this lesson helped you in anyway?

10. What do you like most about yourself? Dislike most about yourself?

11. What makes me happy to be me?

12. What positive things do my family & friends say about me?

13. How can I love myself more?

14. What are some nice things I can give and do for myself daily?

Self Esteem Section

In this section you will need to take some time to write out all of your great qualitties and characteristics. Write out the things that make you happy to be you. You can also take some time to write out good things that your family and friends say about you as well. The better you feel about yourself, the easier it will be for you to feel that you deserve everything that you ask for.

Read this section everday.

Self Esteem

_____
_____
_____
_____
_____
_____
_____
_____
_____
_____
_____
_____
_____
_____
_____
_____
_____
_____
_____
_____
_____
_____
_____
_____
_____
_____

Self Esteem

_____
_____
_____
_____
_____
_____
_____
_____
_____
_____
_____
_____
_____
_____
_____
_____
_____
_____
_____
_____
_____
_____
_____
_____

Self Esteem

Self Esteem

Self Esteem

" WHERE THE MIND GOES THE BODY FOLLOWS.

———

Randolhpy Wilkerson

Chapter Five

Health

Health Section

Our bodies and our health are often times a direct reflection of how well we take care of ourselves. Our bodies are extremely important instruments that take care of us on auto pilot. They do not require a lot from us, only that we eat properly, drink water, and exercise on a regular basis. Without our bodies, where would our spirits live? It is very important to take great care of ourselves and love our bodies unconditionally. If you have abused your body in any way, now is the time to change and begin treating your body like it is priceless, because it is. Without it, you can not survive. Below are a few questions for you to consider before moving forward with your affirmations, journaling, and pictures.

1. Am I healthy?

2. How important is my health and body to me?

3. Am I an emotional eater?

4. Do I give my body everything it needs including love?

5. How often do I show my body appreciation?

6. On a scale from 1-10 how fit am I?

7. What is my ideal body image?

8. What do I want to change about my health?

9. What do I want to change about my body?

10. What changes do I need to make in order to transform my health and my body into what I want?

Health

Health

Health

_____
_____
_____
_____
_____
_____
_____
_____
_____
_____
_____
_____
_____
_____
_____
_____
_____
_____
_____
_____
_____
_____
_____
_____
_____

Health

Health

"

YOU CAN NOT BELONG TO ANYONE ELSE UNTIL YOU BELONG TO YOUR SELF.

———

Pearl Bailey

Chapter Six

Relationships

Relationship Section

The relationships that we have with ourselves are normally a direct reflection of the relationships we have with others. They are mirrors for us. They show us parts of ourselves that we are sometimes blinded to. Relationships are also there to teach us very important lessons that are vital to our growth and development as spirits on the earth plane. Relationships should nuture your growth as well as the other person's growth. If only one of you is benefiting from the relationship then you may want to reassess the relationship you are currently in. If a relationship is not helping you grow then let it go and move forward so that you can make room for another with whom you both can help each other grow. Also, as with the law of attraction, focus only on the qualities that you want in a mate. If you are currently in a relationship with someone then focuses only on what you admire about this person. As a parent or a child, focus only on the qualities that you admire and visualize your relationship with the person the way you would like it to be.

1. How is your relationship with yourself? Your mate? Your family? Your coworkers/Boss?

2. What would you like to change about your relationship with your self? Your family? Your children? Your co workers/Boss?

3. How does your mate make you feel?

4. How do you feel when you are alone?

5. What do you admire most about your self? Your mate? Your chil dren? Your co-workers/boss?

6. What type of relationship did your parents have? Your grandparents?

7. What is your ideal relationship with yourself? Your mate? Your chil dren? Your co-workers/boss?

8. Do you make your partner feel loved, cared about, and appreciated?

9. What have you learned about past relationships or do you keep get ting in the same type of relationships that have the same end result?

10. Do you blame yourself for failed relationships or for the way your partner treats you? If so, why?

Relationships

_____
_____
_____
_____
_____
_____
_____
_____
_____
_____
_____
_____
_____
_____
_____
_____
_____
_____
_____
_____
_____
_____

Relationships

_____
_____
_____
_____
_____
_____
_____
_____
_____
_____
_____
_____
_____
_____
_____
_____
_____
_____
_____
_____
_____
_____
_____
_____

Relationships

_____
_____
_____
_____
_____
_____
_____
_____
_____
_____
_____
_____
_____
_____
_____
_____
_____
_____
_____
_____
_____
_____
_____
_____

Relationships

_____
_____
_____
_____
_____
_____
_____
_____
_____
_____
_____
_____
_____
_____
_____
_____
_____
_____
_____
_____
_____
_____
_____
_____

Relationships

"

IT IS THE FATHERS GOOD PLEASURE TO GIVE YOU THE KINGDOM.

Luke 12:32

Chapter Seven

Finances

Finances Section

Affirm "The Creator's wealth flows to me in great avalanches of abundance."

Do you believe any of the following things?

1. Money Doesn't Grow on trees

2. I am always in Debt

3. Money Goes out Faster than it comes in

4. Money is evil, dirty, and filthy

5. I cant charge that much for my services/products

6. A penny saved is a penny earned

7. Money only comes from hard work

8. I resent people who have lots of money

9. Never lend money

10. I'm not good enough to make money

If so, you HAVE to change your beliefs in order to ProsperFinancially

Our finances are an extremely vital part of all of our lives. We must make money in order to provide for our families, pay our debts, and survive. Financial Freedom is a goal that most want to obtain at some point in their lives. With financial freedom, you can leave your job, travel the world, and give your children the lifestyle you want them to have, be free from financial worries, and have the freedom to do what you want when you want. Remember that money is energy just like you. You can have as much or little as your energy will allow. In this section we are going to focus on money. Here are some questions you should consider before proceeding.

1. What does Financial Freedom mean to me?

2. What is my current financial status?

3. How do I plan on creating Financial Freedom?

4. What are my current thoughts about my finances?

5. What is my current Belief System about Money?

6. Do I believe that I deserve to be financially free?

7. What can I do to create more wealth in my life?

8. What am I constantly affirming about money?

9. How much money do I want to make monthly/daily/weekly/yearly?

10. What will I do with this money once I receive it?

Tips for Creating More Wealth

1. Affirm Daily that you deserve to be wealthy

2. Change your limiting belief system into a limitless belief system

3. Bless Your Bills & Pay them with love and Joy

4. Know that "The Abundance of the Universe is Available to every one"

5. Be Happy for others with Money instead of being Resentful

6. Give Charity Graciously

7. Daily Exercise: Sit with your arms open and affirm, " I am open and receptive to all the good and abundance in the Universe".

8. Release the Fixed Income Mentality begin to affirm, "I now receive my good from expected and unexpected sources"

Finances

Finances

Finances

Finances

Finances

"

YOU SURVIVED 100,000 OTHER
SPERM TO GET HERE, WHAT
DO YOU MEAN YOU DON'T
KNOW WHAT TO DO?

———————

Les Brown

Chapter Eight

Career

Career Section

This is what we spend most of our time doing. Our career has a direct impact on our emotional, physical, spiritual, and financial lives. If you are not happy in your career now is the time to really start to think about what you want to spend most of your time doing. It is a good time to reassess your values, your beliefs, your passions, and your dreams. Some of you may have let your dreams go along time ago because life happened. You got married, had kids, and your life became your family. Others of you may have been to afraid to go after your dreams. And yet others of you may have felt that you weren't capable of doing what you wanted to do. It's ok. That's why you are reading this vision journal, and taking the necessary steps to transform your life into the life of your dreams. Take some time to think about what you really wanted as a child or even a young adult. It's your life you can make it happen. Go for it. There is no limit to what you can do, be or have.

Below is your career assessment. Take some time to really think about these questions.

1. What are you really good at?

2. What do you desire more than anything in the world?

3. What would you do with your time if you had all of the money in the world, after you had all of the material possessions you wanted and had traveled to everywhere you've always wanted to go, what would you spend your time doing?

4. What are you passionate about?

5. What angers you about the world that you wish you could change?

6. How can you be of service to others while doing what you love?

7. What do you fear most about embarking on your career?

8. If you decide not to change your career for something that you love will you regret it on your deathbed?

9. On your deathbed, if you don't change your life now, what will you regret?

10. Which one matters more to you, being fearful and doing it anyways, or being on your deathbed and it's too late?

Career

Career

Career

_____
_____
_____
_____
_____
_____
_____
_____
_____
_____
_____
_____
_____
_____
_____
_____
_____
_____
_____
_____
_____
_____
_____
_____

Career

Career

"

TRUE FORGIVENESS IS WHEN
YOU CAN SAY, THANK YOU
FOR THAT EXPERIENCE.

———————

Oprah Winfrey

Chapter Nine

Forgiveness

Forgiveness Section

In this section we recommend that you take some time to think about everything and everyone that you need to forgive. What are some of your past regrets? What are some things that you are angry about? Are you upset with yourself about anything? Do you feel guilty about anything? Do you need to forgive yourself for anything? It is very important that you forgive yourself and others for whatever they or you did intentionally and unintentionally to yourself. When we are angry or holding feelings of guilt within ourselves, we create blockages that do not allow us to utilize our full creative abilities. You must release these blockages if you are to truly be, have, and do what you want. After you have written down the things that you are angry about, guilty about, or need to forgive, accept that you have these feelings, face them, and then release them, because they no longer serve you. Write a few affirmations to begin the healing process and affirm these throughout the day until they become your beliefs.

What is Forgiveness? Forgiveness of self, is learning to let go of what is past, regretful and painful, releasing it, learning the lesson behind it and loving yourself through the process. Forgiveness of others is excepting them as human, realizing that they too are on a journey of self discovery, learning the lesson that they were sent to teach you, and letting them go. Forgiveness can be a very hard thing to do. You feel hurt, betrayed, and emotionally distraught behind your actions or someone else's. But you must forgive in order to move forward to higher level of self understanding and awareness. Once you realize that it was just an experience and it was necessary for you to go through it to learn something vital to your growth and development it's a whole lot easier.

If you can learn to look at things with your spiritual eye instead of with your physical eye I guarantee you that you're while life will become easier for you. Forgiveness means letting go, loving yourself, learning and moving forward. Below is your forgiveness assessment. As always, please take some time to carefully think about these questions, and you may even want to make up some questions for yourself to answer in the process.

1. What does forgiveness mean to me?

2. What am I really angry with myself about? Why?

3. Who am I angry with? Why?

4. What lesson did I learn from the experience?

5. Why haven't I forgiven myself for _____ ?

6. Did I do what I thought was best at the time?

7. Why haven't I forgiven _____ ?

8. What do I need to do in order to heal from this experience?

9. If I don't forgive myself, how will this effect me? Do I believe that I shouldn't make mistakes or that other people shouldn't make mistakes? Should I not forgive myself for making a decision that I wish I could change? Did I learn from that decision?

Forgiveness

Forgiveness

Forgiveness

Forgiveness

Forgiveness

"

HEAL YOUR PAST SO YOUR PRESENT AND FUTURE CAN BE PEACEFUL.

———

Aishah Tatum

Chapter Ten

Blockages

How to Release Blockages Section

How to Release Blockages

Blockages are internal patterns that we have created that hold us back from our greatness. They are created by us as a result of how we think, perceive, and feel about events that occur not only to us but also in our family and the world. It is important to note, that we create our blockages and we destroy our blockages. We can use these internal obstacles as stepping stones or blockades. It is all a matter of perception. Change the way you perceive the situation or event and your entire reality will shift.

The best way to release blockages is to write, read, and say affirmations specific to your blockages. We recommend first identifying your blockages. Some of you may already know the source of your blockages, others may not understand why the things that you want to do, be, or have are not coming to you. You must first locate your hidden belief system which is located in your subconscious mind. While writing your affirmations notice if you feel any resistance or feelings of uneasiness. If you are, this is where you need to start to identify your hidden beliefs. Write down the thoughts or feelings that you are having when you feel uneasy while voicing or writing your affirmations. After you have done that, write affirmations that will cancel out these beliefs and continue to say these affirmations until you no longer feel resistance.

Blockages

Blockages

Blockages

_____
_____
_____
_____
_____
_____
_____
_____
_____
_____
_____
_____
_____
_____
_____
_____
_____
_____
_____
_____
_____
_____

Blockages

Blockages

"

ALL THAT A MAN ACHIEVES OR FAILS TO ACHIEVE IS THE DIRECT RESULT OF HIS OWN THINKING.

―――――

James Allen

Chapter Eleven

My Accomplishments

My Accomplishments Section

In this section, write down all of the things you are proud of that you have accomplished and revisit this list as often as you need to. It is very important to make a list of all of the great achievements you have had during this life time as well as all of your successes. This not only provides you with encouragement, but it shifts your energy. You can always turn to this section and remind yourself of the wonderful things you have done. Please include accomplishments that had a personal significance for you not just for others.

My Accomplishments

My Accomplishments

My Accomplishments

My Accomplishments

My Accomplishments

"

TO BE WHO YOU ARE AND BECOME WHAT YOU ARE CAPABLE OF IS THE ONLY GOAL WORTH LIVING.

———————

Alvin Ailey

Chapter Twelve

My Life Vision

My Life Vision

In this section take some time to think about the vision you have for your life.

What are your life accomplishments?

Describe in detail where you are in 1 year, 5 years, 10 years, 20 years from now?

Besides your goals for this year, what are some milestone achievements you want to reach or do in your life?

Maybe climb Mount Everest, Visit a tribe in South America?

Build a School or a Hospital overseas?

Maybe travel all seven continents?

Write down lifetime goals in this section in as much detail as possible.

My Life Vision

My Life Vision

My Life Vision

My Life Vision

My Life Vision

Quotes

Self

Self hate is a form of mental slavery that results in poverty, ignorance, and crime

SUSAN TAYLOR

Forgiveness

As soon as healing takes place go out and heal somebody else

MAYA ANGELOU

Life Assessments

Predict lifes alternatives now

IYANLA VANZANT

Financial

If you fall, fall on your back. If you can look up, you can get up.

LES BROWN

Life Vision

I am the thinker that creates the thoughts, that creates the things.

DR. JOHNNIE COLEMAN

Spirituality

Everything that has happened had to happen. Everything that must happen cannot be stopped

DWAYNE DYER

Career

Life has two rules, 1. never quit. 2. always remember rule number 1.

DUKE ELLINGTON

Self

The bumble bees wings are so thin and its body to big, it should not be able to fly. The only problem is, the bees doesn't know that.

DAVID LINDSEY

Spirituality

Faith without work cannot be called faith

THE BIBLE

Mental Strength

LENT= Lets Eliminate Negative Thinking Earl Nightingale
For to whom much is given of him, much shall be expected

LUKE 12:48

Fewness of words greatness of days

ABDUL BAHA

Legacy

Men build institutions that four hundred years later their descendents can say, " He left that".

NA'IM AKBAR

The one who asks questions never loses his way

AKAN PROVERB

Mental Strength

In the providence of the mind, what one believes to be true either is true or becomes true

JOHN LILLY

Life Vision

Your world is as big as you make it

GEOGIA DOUGLAS JOHNSON

Self Confidence

You must act as if it is impossible to fail

ASHANTI PROVERB

Self

A strong man masters other's, a truly wise man masters himself

THE WISDOM OF THE TAOIST

Self

You will never know who you are in the world until you know thyself

DR.JOHN HENRY CLARKE

Spirituality

As long as you can find someone else to blame for anything you are doing, you cannot be held accountable or responsible for your growth or the lack of it.

SUN BEAR

Blockages

You can not fix the problem if you will not face it

JAMES BALDWIN

Life Assessment

If you always do what you always did you will always get what you always got

JACKIE MOMS MABLEY

Life Vision

Strategy is better than strength

HAUSA PROVERB

Spirituality

Although the face of God is before all people the fool can not find it.

THE HUSIA

Principles

A man who stands for nothing will fall for nothing

MALCOM X

Spirituality

The spirit indeed is willing but the flesh is weak

MATTHEW 26:41

Goal Setting

There are three types of people in this world, those who make things happen, those who watch things happen, those who wonder what happened

UNKNOWN

Knowledge

Education is your passport to the future, for tomorrow, belongs to the people who prepare for it today

MALCOM X

Knowledge

Ones work may be finished one day, but ones education never

ALEXANDER DUMAS

The tongue of a man is his sword

THE HUSIA

Principles

Deal with yourself as an individual worthy of respect and make everyone else deal with you the same way

NIKKI GIOVANI

Life Vision

Where you will sit when you are old shows where you stood in youth

YORUBA PROVERB

Principles

Don't let anyone steal your spirit

SINBAD

Principles Spirituality

Keep thy heart with all diligence for out of it are the issues of life

PROVERBS 4:23,24

Life Vision

"You create your own reality. Its not just actions that determine our reality, its our thoughts and beliefs. We have been taught that things happen to us when in fact they happen because of us. Many blame their misfortunes on God, fate, and luck. If you want to find the true master of your fate, look no further than your own mirror. "

– SETH THROUGH JANE ROBERTS

Personal Development

If you don't design your own life plan, chances are you'll fall into someone else's plan. And guess what they have planned for you? Not much

JIM ROHN

Don't wish it were easier, wish you were better.

JIM ROHN

"The tragedy of life is what dies inside a man while he lives."

ALBERT SCHWEITZER

Daily Tracker

Appendix

Daily Tracker:

Track your daily progress towards acheving your goals.

Ideas:

New ideas that come to mind.

Challenges:

What obstacles am I currently facing?

Personal Development:

Who am I becoming?

Daily Tracker

"Discipline is the bridge between goals and accomplishment."

JIM ROHN

Daily Tracker

"Discipline is the bridge between goals and accomplishment."

JIM ROHN

Daily Tracker

"Discipline is the bridge between goals and accomplishment."

JIM ROHN

Daily Tracker

"Discipline is the bridge between goals and accomplishment."

JIM ROHN

Daily Tracker

"Discipline is the bridge between goals and accomplishment."

JIM ROHN

New Ideas

New Ideas Section

New Ideas Section

New Ideas Section

New Ideas Section

New Ideas Section

Challenges

What obstacles am i currently facing?

How am i going to overcome it?

Challenges

Challenges

Challenges

Challenges

Challenges

Personal Development

Who am I becoming?

Personal Development Section

What do I really want to achieve this month, within the next 6 months, this year?

What is my ideal vision of myself? Who do I want to be become overall?

What is my plan of action to becoming the person I want to be?

What is my plan of action to achieving my goals?

Am I making the right decisions to get me where I really want to be?

Am I doing all I can and taking the action necessary to achieve the above objectives?

What Books Should I read to take me to the next level?

What Classes should I Take or have always wanted to take?

What Seminars should I Attend to help move my life forward in the direction of my dreams?

Personal Development

Personal Development

Personal Development

Personal Development

Personal Development

Personal Development

Made in the USA
Lexington, KY
26 September 2019